CHRIST AND ROOTS

JESUS AS REVEALED IN THE BIBLE AND AFRICAN TRADITIONAL RELIGIONS

SECOND EDITION

DR. JOHN G. GITHIGA

Books Academy LLC
112 SW H K Dodgen Loop,
Temple, Texas 76504
Hotline: (254) 800-1189

Ordering Information:
Quantity sales. Special discounts are available on quantity purchases by corporations, associations, and others. For details, contact the publisher at the address above.

Printed in the United States of America.

ISBN-13: Softcover   978-1-964929-60-6
          eBook   978-1-964929-59-0

Library of Congress Control Number: 2024921869

ABOUT THE BOOK

Christ and Roots is about Christ Jesus, who revealed himself to me when I was six years old, about how Jesus talked about himself in the seven "I am" statements in the Gospel according to John, and how the New Testament writers experienced him and wrote about him. It is also about preexistent Christ who revealed himself to the African people long before the missionaries came to Africa. However, we assert that the revelation in Christ Jesus is superior to the one in pre-Christian religions. We fully agree with Hebrews: "In the past God spoke to our ancestors through the prophets at many times and in various ways, but in these last days he has spoken to us by his Son, whom he appointed heir of all things and through whom he also made the universe. The Son is the radiance of God's glory and exact representation of his being, sustaining all things by his powerful word. After he has provided purification for our sins, he sat down at the right hand of Majesty in heaven. So, he became as much as superior to the angels as the name he has inherited is superior to theirs" (Hebrews 1:1–4).

Table of Contents

PREFACE

I delivered my first sermon when I was six years old when I was shepherding with a friend of mine at Ichichi. I started by telling my friend to close his eyes and look at the sun. He did it. I then asked him whether he was seeing anything. He told me that he was not seeing anything. I then started my story:

Last night I was sleeping in a very dark room. There appeared a Being of light and I was scared, so I closed my eyes so that I may not see him. After closing my eyes, I continued seeing the Being of Light. I then covered my eyes with a blanket, but continued seeing the Being. I then covered my eyes with both the blanket and palm of my hand, but the Being remained visible. Eventually, the Being disappeared and left me with unspeakable peace.

I believe this is the same being who appeared to Paul on Damascus road.[1] He says that around noon, "Suddenly a bright light from heaven flashed around me. I fell to the ground and I heard a voice say to me, 'Saul! Saul! Why do you persecute me?'" Unlike Paul, I didn't hear the voice, I was not knocked down, and I was not blinded. But both Paul and I would agree that the light of this Being was brighter than sunlight. He is the one who claimed: "I am the light of the world."[2] He is the one who was, and who is and who is to come.[3] He is one with God who revealed Himself to Moses in the fire, which was in a bush.[4] He is I AM THAT I AM.[5]

Our precious Savior revealed himself again to me at night in the East

African Revival Fellowship that was held in the home of Harriet Evan at Ichichi Village on July 13, 1958. I confessed my sin. The greatest sin and the only sin I remember confessing is blasphemy. This happened when I was eleven. Our mother was tortured during the interrogation by Home

Guard members, who were British Royalists.[6] She was bitten and her thumbnail was broken. Brother Gideon and I were the first to meet Mother as she was crying with pain, currying the little food that our elder sister Jael had prepared for her. Gideon was hungry so he grumbled, took the food, and ate. I was so angry with God that I faced the sky and asked God, "You call yourself a Great Provider (that is the meaning of *Ngai*, a Kikuyu name for God). Is this what you have provided us?" When I repented of my sin, God graciously forgave me and filled me with the Holy Spirit.

As I grew in grace, I learned that God's angels provided for us and protected us during those difficult times. It was a military nurse who treated my mom's injuries by the Home Guard. So after conversion, I experience God as Great Provider, Savior, Redeemer, and Creator who is loving, merciful, and gracious. He is our loving Father who is in control and has our best interest at heart.

I was spiritually nurtured by my brothers and sisters in fellowship as well as by so many other loving pastors and theological educators. I had the blessing of studying in theological colleges for eleven years. My educators included African, Canadian, British, Scottish, Hungarian, Dutch, and Austrian theologians. They all prepared me for a ministry to all the people of God, including ministry to African Americans. From David Philpot, a Scotsman, I learned African theology and black theology, which was useful to the ministry to the African Americans for whom I started ministering when I was a student in the School of Theology of the University of the South from 1976 to 1981. I was first assigned to do a practical internship at St. Mary the Virgin in Chattanooga, where I ministered every Sunday.

I was then led by the Spirit to start a fellowship for the African Americans doing manual work at the university. None of the participants had a college degree. We named the fellowship "Each One Teach One" since Mary and I wanted to learn from the participants as much as they would learn from us. We did. We started teaching with the Gospel of John. We started learning African American culture. One of our surprises was learning that when we were visiting homes, so as to form the group, no man was willing to go with us. And whenever we found a man in the house, we tried to engage him in conversation, but we didn't succeed. When we called those who became close to us, the wife would hold the phone and she would speak for the man. Our sisters talked loud. And if the man tried to ask a question, he was shouted down. Among other things, the study group discussed our prejudices using the story of Nathaniel as a guide. Philip reported to Nathaniel that, "We have found the one Moses wrote about in the law, and about whom the prophets wrote—Jesus of Nazareth, the son of Joseph."[7]

Nathaniel responded, "Nazareth! Can anything good come from there?"[8] I asked the group to discuss our prejudices. To my dismay, they all told me that they don't have prejudices and that Jimmy Carter was the only person who had prejudice. This was contrary to the Jimmy Carter I knew. President Carter was a man of noble character, a committed and born-again Christian who, after his retirement, taught Sunday school in his church.

In the course of time, we attracted a white lady and she decided to join us. When she knocked at the door she was met by the lady of the house with the question, "Why have you come?"

"I am coming for Bible study;" she responded.

And after a serious look, she was let in. To our greatest joy, she stayed in the group until our departure for Kenya. Surprisingly, even after being with our American brothers and sisters for three months, they still believed they could not pronounce our names. One Sunday we attend a black church as a group. Our leader introduced me this way. "I know he is our Bible study leader, and that he come from Kenya, but I cannot figure out his name."

After being with them for three years, they mastered our names and our English fashion. And when we were biding them farewell, they had a big question for me: "Where shall we get another you?"

"The Lord will provide," I responded. Coming back eight years later, I was disappointed to learn that no other seminarian had volunteered to minister with them.

While I was in a Doctor of Ministry program, I met Dr. Herbert Vandort, who was ministering with St. Cyprian's Church in Pensacola, Florida. During the holidays, he invited me to go to minister in his church. Hence, we became friends with this lovely congregation. Most members were professionals. When I returned to Kenya, they communicated with me constantly, asking me to come to minister with them. After five years, I became fully convinced that it was God's call. To be attuned to a parochial ministry, I requested Bishop George Njuguna of the Diocese of Mount Kenya South to place me in one of his parishes for one year before I went to the United States. He graciously placed me at Karura Parish, which had seven churches and a total of three thousand parishioners. As a letter from the bishop states, we had a fruitful ministry. We started several programs that were in preparation for the ministry at St. Cyprian's in Pensacola. My greatest dream was to be in a place where I could write theological books for both Western and African churches. This was fueled by students who boycotted my class because I could not recommend a book on pastoral theology written by an African theologian.

And thus, God granted me the desire of my heart and placed me to minister to an affluent congregation.

1 Acts 9: 3–4.

2 John 8:12.

3 Revelation 1:4.

4 Exodus 3:2.

5 Exodus 3:14.

6 The Home Guard consisted of Kenyans loyal to the Colonial government of Great Britain during the turbulent years leading up to Kenya independence.

7 John 1:45.

8 John 1:46.

ACKNOWLEDGMENTS

Since the sermon draws from the whole of the preacher's life, my gratitude goes to all who contributed to my spiritual and professional growth. I am most grateful to my father, the late Isaac Githiga, from whom I learned the art of preaching when I was still in my mother's womb. I don't remember how many times I have preached on my father's last text "but as many has received him, to them he gave power to become the sons of God, to them that believe on his name." As it was with my father, the phrases "In Christ," "by Christ," and "for Christ" are central to my preaching. My gratitude also goes to my mother, Joyce Njeri Githiga, for communicating to me the attributes of God at the earliest stage of my life.

Tremendous thanks go out to Mary Nyambura, my wife, for encouraging me and producing a conducive environment for writing and preaching.

Big thanks to Dr. Glen Sanborn, Dr. Elizabeth Larson, and our son, Isaac Cyprian Githiga, for proofreading the manuscript.

INTRODUCTION

Christ and Roots grew out of sermons delivered at St. Cyprian's Episcopal Church of the Diocese of Central Gulf Coast. St. Cyprian's is comprised of professional black people, most of whom are in the teaching profession. Others are technicians and leaders in various sectors of the city of Pensacola

Since Christ is the author of our salvation, the focal point of our faith and mission, I felt urged by the Holy Spirit to start preaching about who Jesus is. Moreover, Christ has been the greatest Being in my life ever since I was confronted by him when I was fifteen years of age. For me, therefore,

Christology[2] is fundamental to our preaching and theology. Indeed, theology is Christology and Christology is theology. It precedes

soteriology[10] in that we are confronted with Jesus first, and then we respond to him by faith. After this response, we start speaking about God. "For man believes with his heart and so he is justified, and he confesses with his lips

and so he is saved"[11]

I should also admit that I am a minister of the Gospel and a theologian only because Christ dwells in me and me in him. Preaching and writing, therefore, is a part of my confession. It is a proclamation of the Being from whom I experience the greatest riches, the greatest peace, and the greatest joy. Since St. Cyprian's family is very dear to me, I felt compelled to start by sharing with them my knowledge and experience of this precious and ineffable Being.

I commenced with the "I am" statements of Jesus, for these sayings present a highly exalted Christ of Johannine meditation. John, by using symbols that were prevalent in his time, reveals the eternal word (*Logos*) in a unique way. He depicts him as "I am that I am" who revealed himself to Moses in a burning bush. He portrays him as "I am who I have been, who I know am, and who will be in the future." He is the one who is, who was, and who is come. He transcends time and space, and he is the ground of our being.

Christ and Roots uses traditional African propositions about the pre- existent Christ as the means of bringing home to my hearers (and now readers) the truth about the Christ of the New Testament. Just as it is difficult to distinguish between Christ of Faith and Jesus of Nazareth, it is also impossible to distinguish between pre-existent Christ and the Christ of the New Testament. This pre-existent Christ, as we shall note in the coming chapters, was evident in African religions just as he was evident in Judeo- Greco-Roman religions.

It is very interesting to note that there are three threads interwoven in the "I am" sayings of Jesus. They all express Christ's self-knowledge, self- giving, and intimacy. "I am the bread of life, he who come to me shall not hunger, and he who believes in me shall not thirst."[12]

Because he is the life-giving water, he invites us to drink of this water. "Whoever drinks of the water that I shall give him will never thirst; the water that I shall give him will become in him a spring of water welling up to eternal life."[13]

<u>9</u> Christology is generally defined as that part of Christian theology related to the person, nature, and role of Christ.

<u>10</u> The study of salvation doctrines.

<u>11</u> Romans 10:10.

<u>12</u> John 6 35.

<u>13</u> John 4:14.

CHAPTER ONE

The Life-Giving Water

I have a life-giving water—come and drink.

—John 4:1–16

IF YOU VISITED THE MARTIN Luther King Center[1], you would see many symbols showing the life and work of one of the greatest saints of the twentieth century. In the archives of the center, you would see Dr. King's handwritten sermons, which reveals him as a great preacher. You would see an old worn-out Bible, which indicates that King had a deep love for the word of God. You would see his doctoral gown, which shows that he was a learned person.

But the most compelling symbol is the water that surrounds his grave. This water signifies life, death, and rebirth. The designers and architects of the graveyard seem to have drawn heavily from the African collective unconscious. For Africans, water symbolizes life, rebirth, new beginning, and beauty.

Customarily, if someone was seriously ill, and to the point of fainting, Africans would pour water on him in order to restore his life.

Water was also essential for initiation. One of the initiation rituals included bathing in cold running water. The meaning behind this ritual was to cleanse and to wash away the past life in order to prepare the candidates for a new beginning.

Interestingly, the Bible connects the water with the beginning. The first paragraph of the Bible states, "In the beginning God created the heavens and the earth. The earth was without form and void and the darkness was upon the face of the deep; and the *Spirit of God was moving over the face of the waters*" (Genesis 1:2). Here, the water is put at the root of the universe and is depicted as God's pathway.

Water is necessary for Christian initiation. In the Rite of Baptism, the water symbolizes cleansing of sin, death, resurrection, rebirth, and incorporation to the Christian family. Christ is reminding us that he is the living water.

The phrase "living water" has a double meaning. It is used for stream water as opposed to stagnant water. Stream water was used by Africans for initiation. In a deeper meaning, the word points to the life-giving water, which is the precious quality of the Godhead, which fills our spiritual vacuums and gives us love and the peace that passes all understanding. If we are imbued with this substance, we will not need drugs or alcohol in order to be high.

I would like to draw your attention to four points related to Christ as the giver of the water of life.

1. *He is the life-giving water to both the Samaritans and the Jews.* As John 4:9 indicates, the Jews did not associate with the Samaritans. "They will not use the same cups and bowls that the Samaritans use" (John 4:9).

   Put in the modern terms and within our context, the Jews and the Samaritans could not board the same bus, use the same bathroom, attend the same school, or worship in the same church. The two peoples shared an abhorrent racial prejudice. Don't we still experience this ruinous, racial prejudice in this society?

When I first wrote the sermon upon which this chapter is based, I recalled a then recent issue of the *Pensacola Voice* that had an article by Lynda Couture entitled "A New Reality-Coloring Coding Man."[2] The author contends that for Color Coding Man: "White represents better, more capable, easier to train, more trustworthy, and higher caliber. Black represents lazy, less capable, inferior, loose morals, conniving, and limited." This coding has a devastating effect on human relationships. It puts you in an awkward situation whereby you are suspected, belittled, and avoided purely on the color of your skin. This coding, as Lynda rightly argues, is on both sides (white and black).

If we drink the life-giving water, we will be aware of the fact that we (black and white) share the same humanity with similar strengths and limitations. We share the same air, the sun, the rain, and similar human feelings. We are all created in the image of God. Indeed, if we wade into the life-giving water we will realize that we came and that we will leave this world in the same manner (birth/death), no matter what color our skin is.

The same earth is our home. The same God is our Father and, for that reason, we must have equal rights and opportunities.

Thus, if the life-giving water flows in human life, there must be intimate relationships between male and female, young and old, rich and poor, white and black.

2. *Jesus, the life-giving water, creates a dialogue where there is no communication.* There was no communication between the Jews and the Samaritans, but Christ, the Messiah, established a dialogue between him and the Samaritan woman.[3] If we allow this water to flow in our lives, it will facilitate a positive dialogue, which results in friendship and love. There is a Kikuyu love song that states: "To talk is to love; to keep silence

is to foster hatred." This implies that communication is love and love is communication. Positive communication is an effective medication to a sick person. In the words of C. G. Jung: "Therapy is dialogue and dialogue is therapy."[4]

3. *We can draw this life-giving water without a bucket.* In this country, we may not understand the importance of a bucket for drawing water. We may not even realize the importance of water, since to get the water all you need to do is turn a tap and the water comes out.

    At my former parish in Kenya, most families depended on water from the well. At every well there was a bucket tied with the long rope for dipping and pulling the bucket. Should there be no bucket, there could be no water for animal and human life. However, Jesus is talking about spiritual water. This water can be acquired without a natural means. You don't have to be macho, exceptionally wise, educated, or wealthy to be able to draw this water. All that is required of you is to open your mouth wide and God will fill you with the water of life.

4. *The life-giving water guides us to all the truth.* Jesus, in his dialogue with the Samaritan woman, led her to a deep truth—the truth about herself and the truth about God. She was enabled to turn to herself.

"Go and bring your husband," said Jesus. "I don't have a husband," she answered.

"You are right when you say that you don't have a husband," Jesus responded. "You have been married to five men and the man you live with now is not really your husband. You have told me the truth" (John 4:16–18).

Jesus made her more aware of her sexual relationship. Consequently, she discovered that Jesus was Messiah. This led her to a deep truth about God.

She became cognizant of the fact that true worship is worship in the Spirit. "God is Spirit," said Jesus, "and only by the power of his Spirit can people worship him as he really is" (John 4:24). This implies that true worship opens all the windows of our beings, so that the Holy Being may fill us with the life-giving water.

This message poses deep and far-reaching questions to us. If Jesus is the life-giving water to both the Jews and the Samaritans, why is all the human garbage projected on the "Samaritans," the blacks, while the clean part of humanity is projected on the "Jews," the whites? How long will the blacks be disparaged by both whites and blacks? Why are these sons and daughters of the King depreciated day in and day out? How long will human supremacy be projected to our white brothers and sisters—by both whites and blacks—and thereby making them suffer from an inflated ego? When shall we be fully conscious of the fact that we are all created in the image of God? How can we improve our means and methods of communication? How can we enhance a positive dialogue among us? Are our souls watered by the life-giving water? If so, why don't we grow? Why don't we wade in the precious water moment by moment?

Wade in the water.

Wade in the water.

Wade in the water.

God's a-going to trouble the water. [5]

---

1 Located in Atlanta, Georgia, the Dr. Martin Luther King, Jr. National Historic Site has several buildings, including Rev. King's boyhood home and the original Ebenezer Baptist Church, the church where both he and his father were pastors. Dr. Martin Luther King, Jr.'s gravesite and a reflecting pool are located next to Freedom Hall.

<u>2</u> The *Pensacola Voice* was established in 1963 to serve as the voice of the African-American community. As of December 2016, its website is at: pensacolavoice.com.

<u>3</u> John 4:1–42.

<u>4</u> Analytical or Jungian psychology is based upon the ideas of Dr. Carl Gustav Jung, a Swiss psychiatrist (1875–1961). Jungian analysis emphasizes the importance of unconscious influences on one's current emotional state that interfere with living a full and satisfying life. Analysis is a joint effort by two people to try to understand the impact of these unconscious influences on behavior, relationships, and feelings. The role of the analyst is to help the client understand himself or herself, especially the unrecognized or unacknowledged aspects of personality. For a review of Jungian analysis, See Dr. Paul Smerz, "Jungian Analysis," on-line at: http://www.drpaulsmerz.org/jungian-analysis-in-milwaukee/jungian-analysis.

<u>5</u> "Wade in the Water," is an African-American spiritual. According to Dr. C. Michel Hawn, University Distinguished Professor of Church Music and director of the sacred music program in Perkins School of Theology, Southern Methodist University, water is an important image in the African-American spiritual. He explains, "Deep River, My Home Is Over Jordan" is a song that finds hope on the other side of the river. "Go Down, Moses" is a spiritual of deliverance in which Pharaoh's armies were drowned in the sea. Water was a primary aspect of slave experience. Africans began their captivity—the "middle passage"—by traveling across the ocean to a new land in slave ships. See C. Michael Hawn, History of Hymns: "Wade in the Water," on-line at https://www.umcdiscipleship.org/resources/history-of-hymns-wade-in-the-water.

CHAPTER TWO

The Bread Of Life

I am the bread of life—come and dine.

—John 6:22–58

IN THIS "I AM," CHRIST is revealed as the great Provider and sustainer of the human life. The conception of God as the provider and the sustainer is central to the African belief. The most common name of God among the Kikuyu, for instance, is *Ngai,* which can be interpreted as *the great provider.* The Kikuyu,[6] as it is with other African people, believe that all we have, and all that we are, except sin, is God given. Ngai is the source of all that which is wonderful and inexplicable. This is well-articulated by a Kikuyu proverb: "All what we have is provided for by the one who dwells in the sky."

The African people conceived God as one who meets the needs of his creatures. God is the source of rain, life and health, and other necessities needed for sustaining the creation. For that reason, he is addressed to as the rain giver, the water giver, or the great one of the forest.

Thus Jesus's statement "I am the bread of life" connects him with the divine providence. It is in keeping with the ancient myths that associated the divinity with food. Babylonian myth, for instance, had an idea of heavenly bread. The Greeks had an idea about the "food of the gods." The Jews, who expected a second or eschatological manna, believed that as the first redeemer, Moses caused manna[7] to come from heaven; so it would be with the last redeemer.

In the wisdom literature,[8] the wisdom is described as the bread: "she will nourish him with the bread of understanding and give him water of learning to drink." Philo[9] also taught that manna is a type of the *Logos*, which nourishes the soul. Thus, the words *bread* or *food* could convey a profound meaning to John's readers.

Jesus reminds us: "I am the bread of life, he who comes to me will never hunger" (John 6:35). He is claiming to be the source of spiritual energy. He is not only the sustainer but a dynamic power that enables us to overcome the evil powers. In the words of Martin Luther King, Jr., "At the center of Christian faith is the conviction that in the universe, there is a God of power who is able to do exceedingly abundant things in the nature and in history."[10]

Jesus's claim is within the context of feeding the five thousand.[11] This sign was to manifest Christ as the great provider who fed the Israelites with manna in the wilderness.[12] However, the five thousand didn't grasp the

meaning behind the miracle. Jesus, therefore, tries to draw them to a deeper

meaning. He wanted them to know that Christ, like the divine wisdom, will nourish them with the bread of understanding and give them the water of learning to drink. "Do not work for the food that perishes." He challenges them. "Instead, work for the food that lasts for eternal life" (John 6:27). Jesus was telling them, don't come for the bread that you ate yesterday, but come for the spiritual food. It is the food that nourishes the soul and gives it energy and will for doing God's work. This food includes believing in him whom God has sent.

The multitude didn't understand what Jesus was up to. They wanted Jesus to become Moses, who they thought gave the Israelites manna in the wilderness. They thought that the answer to their present situation was to be found in their past. Many a time when the present becomes hopeless, we idolize our past. We make an attempt to return to the paradise that was lost. More often than not, this paradise never existed.

Jesus, on the other hand, brought home to those who would hear the truth of the past. "It was not Moses who gave you the manna, but God" (John 6:32). This manna symbolized the real bread. This real bread is God's gift to the world, which is "he who comes from heaven and gives life to the world" (John 6:33).

Jesus's audience still understood him in a superficial way. "Sir," they asked him, "give us this bread always" (John 6:34). Satisfy our hunger instinct always. Give us material things always. There are many who come to church for material benefits. These are people who regard the church as fried chicken rather than the salt of the world. They regard the church as a mere social club rather than a spiritual institution.

Jesus is still drawing their attention to a deeper meaning. "Your ancestors ate manna in the desert, but they died. But the bread that comes down from heaven is of such a kind that whoever eats it will not die. I am the living bread that comes down from heaven. If anyone eats this bread, he will live forever" (John 6:49–50). Here, Christ is referring them to a profound truth. He is talking about God's revelation through Christ. By giving the Israelites bread in the wilderness, Yahweh was revealing himself as an effective presence in the midst of his people. He manifested himself as a great provider and a sustainer. The discourse with the five thousand is also referring to the Eucharistic flesh of Jesus. It reveals not only Christ's presence in the Eucharist but his simultaneous presence among his followers. This is well demonstrated by his farewell words to his disciples: "I am with you always, to the close of this age" (Matthew 28:20). His presence gives us interior resources.

This is an inner energy that Martin Luther King, Jr. described as an "interior resource which enables us to confront the trial and difficulties of life. It enables us to confront the heavy burdens of sorrow and the hurricane forces of the evil one. It is a brilliant light which illuminates our darkest night."[13]

"I am the bread of life," said Jesus. "He who comes to me will never be hungry he who believe in me will never be thirsty" (John 6:35).

---

6 The Kikuyu tribe is a Bantu tribe that neighbors the Embu, Mbeere, and Meru tribes around Mount Kenya. For more information, see the online Kenya Information Guide at: http://www.kenya- information-guide.com/kikuyu-tribe.html.

7 Book of Exodus, chapter 16.

8 The books of Job, Psalms, Proverbs, Ecclesiastes, Song of Songs, Wisdom of Solomon, and Ecclesiasticus. Also known as the Sapiential Books.

9 Philo of Alexandra (20 BC–AD 40)—His works influenced early Christian theologians.

10 See "God Is Able." A Sermon by Dr. Martin Luther King, Jr., edited for today by Charles Henderson. Online as of December 27, 2016 at http://www.godweb.org/godisable.htm.

11 Matthew 14:13–21; Mark 6:30–44; Luke 9:10–17; and John 6:1–15.

12 Exodus 16:14–36.

13 Martin Luther King, Jr., "Our God is Able" in Washington (ed.). A Testament of Hope at p.509. See also, David Neville and Philip Matthews (eds.). *Faith and Freedom: Christian Ethics in a Pluralist Culture*, ATF Press at p.98 (citing to David Neville. "King, Merton and Barth: Their Abiding Significance.")

CHAPTER THREE

The Light Of The World

I am the light of the world—follow me and have the light of life.

—John 8:12, 9:5

ONE OF THE NAMES OF the Kikuyu God is Mwenenyaga. The word refers to the brightness of the snow at the peak of Mount Kenya. Mount Kenya is the highest mountain in Kenya. The snow at the peak is the only snow known to the Kikuyu. Thus, the deeper theological meaning of the Mwenenyaga is "the possessor of the unique light," or "the source of the unique light," or "he who shines in holiness."

As the name connotes, the Kikuyu use the imagery of the "light" for God and his presence. This concept is well delineated by a Kikuyu Christian folk song, which says,

The light on the mountain,

Which illuminates the whole universe.

It beams on the beautiful green pasture

The same light illuminates my heart,

Since the Lord in me shines like the sunbeams.

This song describes Jesus as the Light, which is on the highest mountain. A light that illumines our hearts. A light that shines in other human families. This is the light that has guided God's people everywhere and at all times.

The term *light*, when used for the Supreme Being, points to the essence of God and to all that which is divine and holy. In the Old Testament, this quality of the Godhead is referred to as "a lamp unto my feet, and a light unto my path."(Psalm 119:105) It was this light that led the Israelites in their pilgrimage. It is the same light that guides us through the wilderness of contradictions and meaninglessness.

Today, as always, Jesus reminds us: "I am the light of the world, whoever follows me will have the light of life, and will never walk in darkness"

(John 8:12). This "I am" is within the context of the sign of giving the sight to the blind man. Here, Jesus is depicted as the giver of sight.[14] According to Johannine, platonic ontology, the physical eyesight would point out to the inner and invisible light. The sign of the healing of the blind man teaches us that:

1. *The blind man had a natural blindness.* The disciples thought that the blind man's sickness was caused by either his misdeeds or the misdeeds of his parents. But for Jesus, "His blindness has nothing to do with his sins or his parents' sins. He is blind so that God's power might be seen at work in him" (John 9:3).

   There is a part of our being that suffers from natural and cultural blindness. But if we surrender this realm to Christ, God's glory will be manifested in us.

2. *The blind man was a beggar.* Those people who are spiritually blind tend to lose direction. They have no moral principles. They beg values from society.

   They are constantly influenced by the media. But when their inner life is illumined by the great I-Am-That-I-am, they acquire self-knowledge. They have courage to say "this is me" and "this is not me"; "this is for me" and "this is not for me."

3. *Jesus used a popular medication.* He "spat on the ground and made some mud with the spittle: he rubbed the mud on the man's eyes" (John 9:6). In the ancient world, spittle was regarded as medication.[15] Jesus, therefore, used a popular belief to enhance the faith of the blind man. God uses familiar things and people to facilitate the restoration of our sight. Miracles do not necessarily happen through the supernatural phenomena. God can come to us wearing an ordinary garment. He may come to us wearing blue jeans. But we have to learn to listen and obey him.

4. *The blind man was sent to the pool of Siloam.* Jesus wanted the man to participate in the healing process. He didn't like to do it for him, but to do it with him. This is what we call God and humanity working together. This attitude is central to African Christians. In Kenya, it is common to find vehicles with inscriptions with the following words: "God helps those who help themselves" and "Help me God; Help yourself." In other words, the owner of the automobiles is asking for God's help. At the same time, he challenges himself to play his part. This attitude, which is termed synergy by ascetical theologians, was central to the teaching of the Fathers. Gregory of Nyssa,[16] for instance, maintained that the divine energy and human energy must work together for our spiritual growth. In this double effort, human persons are invited to strive so that the Spirit may manifest himself to them. The human effort is based on faith, and so it is undertaken and carried out by the strength of the Spirit whose manifestation is its goal. This joint working together leads the soul to flower to freedom and supreme beauty.

   Thus, Christ, the light, is challenging us to join hands with him for our salvation. In the words of Paul, Jesus is inviting us to "work out your salvation with fear and trembling for God is at work in you both to will and to work for his good pleasure." (Philippians 2:13)

5. *Through faith, obedience, and involvement, the blind man was healed.* Christ can heal our natural and cultural blindness

through faith. Faith does not emanate from people who know no suffering. Faith is very much connected with suffering. The blind man was a suffering man. He had missed so much in life. The history of the black race is the history of suffering. But this experience ought to make us a community of faith. "Faith," as one Christian writer puts it, "like a jackal, feeds among the tombs, and even from these dead doubts she gathers her most vital hope."[17]

6. *After becoming a child of light he was confronted by the children of darkness.* This confrontation is evident in the Dead Sea Scrolls, which were contemporaneous with the fourth Gospel. In these scrolls, we read about the war between the children of the light and the children of the darkness. According to this writing, the children of the light will overcome. Their victory was yet in the future. Nevertheless, for John: "the light shines in the darkness, and the darkness has not overcome it" (John 1:5). Thus, in Christ Jesus, the light of the world, we are assured of his victorious guidance.

7. *As the child of light, the healed man made an effort of winning others for Christ.* In the heat of confrontation during questioning by the Pharisees and Jewish authorities, a blind man healed by Jesus said, "I do not know if he is a sinner or not. One thing I do know; I was blind, and now I see" (John 9:25). After a long interrogation he asked them, "Why do you want to hear it again? Maybe you, too, would like to be his disciple?" (John 9:27). Those who have seen the light should bring others to the light.

To this end, Christ is reminding us, "I am the light of the world, whoever follows me will have the light of life and will never walk in darkness" (John 8:12).

14 Luke 18:35–43; Mark 8:22–25; Mark 10:46–52; and John 9:1–12.

15 Interestingly, in 2008, scientists in the Netherlands reported identifying a compound in human saliva that greatly speeds wound healing. "Licking Your Wounds: Scientists Isolate Compound In Human Saliva That Speeds Wound Healing." *Science Daily*. On-line as of December 2016 at: https://www.sciencedaily.com/releases/2008/07/080723094841.htm.

16 He was Bishop of Nyssa from 372–376 and from 378 until his passing. As a theologian, he contributed to understanding the Trinity and to the development of the Nicene Creed. He is recognized as a saint by Anglicanism, Eastern Orthodoxy and Roman Catholicism.

17 The quote is from Herman Melville and appears in his novel *Moby Dick* as an observation of a fictional character. One commentator describes the novel as "one of the most aggressively honest explorations of Christianity that emerged from the nineteenth century." See Daniel Siedell. "Melville's Epilogue." Online as of December 2016 at http://www.patheos.com/blogs/cultivare/2012/09/melvilles-epilogue/.

CHAPTER FOUR

The Good Shepherd

I am the good shepherd—I died for you.

—John 10:1–18

A 1986 ISSUE OF *TIME* magazine had an article titled "Nakasone's World- Class Blunder." The article discussed a statement made by Japan's leader that stirred a tempest by linking race and intellect. The then-prime minister said, "So high is the level of our education in our country that Japan's is an intelligent society. Our average score is much higher than those of countries like the U.S. There are many Blacks, Puerto Ricans and Mexicans in America. Consequently, the average score over there is exceedingly low."

While the article expresses the American indignation, which was aroused by the statement, to my surprise, the writer finally agreed with Nakasone that in comparison, the Japanese performance is higher than that of the United States. However, what got on my nerves in the article was the contention that it is ethnic groups that are dragging down the overall American performance. It was irritating to learn from the article that a specialist in education psychology in Japan has a hierarchical arrangement of IQ scores(which might have meant SAT). The color of the skin determines where one is in the scheme:

Whites show the average score	94
of	0
Mexican-Americans	80
	8
Puerto Ricans	77
	7
Blacks	72
	2

The blacks, since they are the darkest, are put at the bottom of the intellectual ladder. The point that Nakasome wanted to make is that Japanese are more intelligent than the American

The Bad Shepherds

The bad shepherds take care of themselves and never tend the sheep. They kill and eat the finest sheep. They don't take care of the ones that are sick. They don't seek the lost. They run away when they see a wolf coming. Their very intention is to steal, kill, and destroy. They can only strengthen their egos by weakening and destroying the ego of the sheep. They feel self- esteem only when they are better off than others. These poor shepherds will drink of the cup of the wrath of God. God will destroy them and God will be the shepherd for his sheep. "I, myself, will search for my sheep, and will seek them out" (Ezekiel 34:15). As the shepherd seeks out his flock when it has been scattered abroad, so will the Lord seek out his flock when it has been scattered abroad, so will the Lord seek out his sheep and will rescue them.

When I first preached the sermon that is the basis of this chapter, I said that the Great Shepherd will one day rescue his black sheep in South Africa. In the words of Bishop Tutu: "O, God, I know we will be free; but why suffer for too long?"[18]

We possibly suffer for too long in order to become the wounded healers.

The Good Shepherds

Christ Jesus is the good Messianic Shepherd who gathers together the scattered sheep. He doesn't entertain exclusive philosophy. He knows that all parts belong to the whole, and the whole can never be the whole if some parts are segregated.

The good shepherd leads the sheep to green pastures. "I will let them graze in safety," he says, "In the mountains, meadows, and valleys and in all the green pastures" (Ezekiel 34:14).

The good shepherd seeks the lost. If one of the hundred sheep got lost, he leaves the other ninety-nine sheep in the pasture and goes looking for the one that got lost, until he finds it.[19]

The good shepherd rescues the sheep from the wolves of psychologically debilitating forces. He says: "I will rescue my sheep and will not let them be mistreated anymore."

This great shepherd will strengthen the sheep's souls so that even if they are attacked, they will not lose their integrity and dignity and self-esteem.

There will be a mutual knowledge between the shepherd and the sheep. He will know them. He will call them by their names and they will follow him. He will approach them as individuals who belong to a particular community, a community with a unique spiritual potentiality born of a peculiar experience.

The good shepherd leads the sheep. He became human in order to show us what God wanted us to be and to do. After his death, resurrection, and ascension, he returned in his spirit. Through his spirit, he leads us to the way of life. In order to be saved, one has to do more than following him. One has to confess with his mouth that Jesus is Lord and ask him to be his Lord and Savior.

The good shepherd gives us life—life in all its fullness. This life comes as a result of knowing and being with God. It is eternal life. "And this is life eternal, that they might know thee, the only true God, and Jesus Christ, whom thou hast sent" (John 17:3). This life, which comes from God through the Good Shepherd, is more than mere existence. It is not just a

survival. In the words of William Ralph Inge[20]: "Eternal life and survival are not the same, and yet, they are related to each other. Survival is a quantitative measure of duration. Eternal life belongs to the conception of reality as a kingdom of values; survival conceives human existence as a page of history." Eternal life is a quality of ultimate reality, which leads to a deeper knowledge about God, self-knowledge, and self-giving.

Thus, Christ is telling us, "I am the good shepherd. The good shepherd lays down his life for the sheep."

---

18 Anglican Bishop Desmond Mpilo Tutu of South Africa was a fierce opponent of apartheid, a system that officially segregated and discriminated on the basis of race. The black sheep were rescued. South Africa abandoned apartheid in 1994.

19 See Matthew 18:12 and Luke 15:4.

20 W. R. Inge." Eternal Life and Survival" in *The Christian Century*. Vol.38, No.2 (July 7, 1921). William Ralph Inge was an English author, Anglican priest, professor of divinity at Cambridge, and Dean of St. Paul's Cathedral in England. He died in 1954.

CHAPTER FIVE

The Door Of The Sheep

I am the door—come in by me and be saved.

—John 10:7, 9

"**I** AM THE DOOR—COME TN by me and be saved." In this statement, Christ is depicted as the door of and for the sheep. The Greek word thyra, which is translated in English as "door," would also mean the "entrance" or "access." This "I am" saying, therefore, depicts Christ as the door for, and an access to, salvation. He draws the sheep to him and also protects them from the wolves.

As it is in the statement, traditionally, the African believed that God is the protector of his people. The Burundi, for instance, call him "Watcher of Everything;" while the Baganda regard him as "The Great Eye." God, who is "The Great Eye," watches everything and protects all that which he has created. Since his protection is universal, the Buganda say: "The plant protected by God is never hurt by the wind." In this regard, the Kikuyu has a proverb which says: "The fire protected by God is kept burning by the banana fibers."

The concept of the gate as the door of salvation is prevalent in the Old Testament. The psalmist sings, "Open to me the gate of the Temple; I will go in and give thanks to the Lord. This is the gate of the Lord; only the righteous can come in" (Psalm 118:19).

By entering through this gate, the psalmist enjoys God's victorious protection. He feels confident and comfortable in the pen of the sheep. Here he experiences God's presence. In God's presence his fear vanishes: "The Lord is with me," he says, "I will not be afraid; what can anyone do to me?" (Psalm 118:6). The psalmist also uses the imagery of gates for the means through which the King of Glory comes in. He confidently shouts, "Fling wide the gates; open the ancient doors and the Great King will come in.

Who is the great King? He is the Lord, strong and mighty, the Lord, victorious in battle" (Psalm 24:7–8). This Old Testament background might have influenced the writer of the fourth Gospel. For him, Christ is the door for the sheep. Through him the Lord of Glory comes in. He who is strong and mighty enters the pen of the sheep (the Church) and lives with the sheep. He is, also, influenced by pre-Christian literature in which the redeemer is compared with the door of the sheep. However, John uses a familiar term to convey a very deep meaning to his readers. For him, Jesus is the absolute door to salvation. Christ alone is the gate to the underserved presence of God. He is the redeemer who is above other redeemers and a mediator who cannot be equated with other mediators. He cannot be equated with the African intermediaries. He is not on the same plane with the Old Testament priests and prophets. He is not one of the archangels. He is uncreated and, therefore, superior to all creation.

Those who belong to him enjoy abundance of life. They enjoy his freedom and protection and providence. "Whoever comes in by me will be saved," says Jesus. "He will come in and go out and find pasture," (John 10:9).

In Christ, we enjoy spiritual freedom. In him, we are in beautiful green pastures, and we are ever assured of God's perpetual sustenance. For "the world and all that is in it belong to the Lord; the earth and all who live on it are his" (Psalm 24:1).

Those who belong to Christ, the door to salvation, know him. They know him because they enter through him and live with and in him. They belong to this precious redeemer, because God chooses them for him. They enjoy God's sustenance, because they have accepted to be in Christ. They, then, follow Christ because God has given them power to do so.

Thus, Christ is reminding us that he is the gate and that if we enter by him, we will be saved. Let us, therefore, ponder today's message with the aid of the question and the answer of the psalmist: " Who may ascend the mountain of the Lord? Who may stand in his holy place? Those who have clean hands and pure heart, who does not trust in idol or swear by a false God." (Psalm 24:4-5).

CHAPTER SIX

The Way Of Life

I am the way—do not be worried.

—John 14:1–14

WE HAVE BEEN LOOKING AT the "I am" sayings of Jesus from our African background. Now, I would like to draw your attention to Christ's claim: "I am the way."

According to the material at my disposal, the Africans never conceived of God as a way to God. This is owing to the fact that the Africans religions were monotheistic. They believed in one God who had many names. In addition, the Africans never spoke of God as one in three persons. And thus, we didn't have a belief in God the Son who could be the way to the Father.

The Africans, however, had intermediaries. They communicated to God through these intermediaries. These intermediaries included their parents, their ancestors, and the divinities. From our childhood, we were trained to honor our parents because through them we could receive either God's blessing or curse. We were also taught to venerate our ancestors, just as we are encouraged to honor the saints by Christian religion. Nevertheless, none of the African intermediaries were ever regarded *the* way to God.

For that reason, the revelation of God in Christ supersedes the revelation we had in African religions. As the Epistle to the Hebrews states, "In the past God spoke to our ancestors many times and in many ways through the prophets, but in these last days, he has spoken to us through his son. He is the one through whom God created the universe, the one whom God has chosen to possess all things..." (Hebrews 1:1–2).

Thus, God the Son is superior to our ancestors. He surpasses the divinities and the angels because the universe was created through and for him. Hence, he has the right to claim: "I am the true and the living way" (John 14:6).

The context within which this statement was made was an atmosphere of worry. The disciples were worried. They were worried because their master was about to leave. As it was with the disciples we, too, worry and get upset. There are external voices that call us to worry. The media is the major external voice. When I first addressed this point in my homily I said:

The media is seducing us to worry about AIDS. It is telling us that by 1991 there will be 270,000 AIDS cases, which will result in 179,000 deaths. We are told that the cost of the medical care for AIDS patients will soar to 16 billion dollars. Each patient will need 46,000 dollars for each treatment. Politicians and businessmen are behind this propaganda. Medical business persons are appealing to our subliminal senses. They want the masses to flock to hospitals for checkups and pay the costly medical bills without complaints. It was stated that AIDS could do for Houston hospitals what heart transplants have done for the Humane Institutes of Kentucky.

I believe the healthcare-related businesses seduce us to worry in order to make money out of our worry.

The media persuades us to worry about the possibility of nuclear holocaust and man-made climate change. We are advised to worry about the yawning gap between the rich and poor. The inner voices could induce us to worry about the future of our children, to worry about our future health, to worry about the impending old age, etc.

The aim of this deadly animal, worry, is to debilitate and just waste our time. I would like to share my weakness with regard to worry. For by sharing my wounds I might heal those who are wounded. But when I share my strength I intimidate those who are weak.

As I was preparing the sermon that became this chapter, some strange voices came, which were persuading me to worry. Finally, I was manipulated by these voices. I then stopped preparing the sermon and spent half of the morning worrying. In the afternoon, I reflected on my worry. I was dismayed at discovering that I had just burned my energy and wasted my time. I gained nothing at all.

Hence, Christ is telling us to set our troubled heart at rest. We should be at peace with ourselves because of the following factors.

Nothing can separate us from **God**. "Who can separate us from the love of God which is ours in Christ Jesus? Can the hardship do it? Can danger or death do it? No!" (Romans 8:35). As Paul said, we have complete victory through him who loved us and for that reason: "neither the world above nor the world below—nothing in all creation will ever be able to separate us form the love of God which is ours in Christ Jesus our Lord" (Roman 8:38– 39).

We should not worry because "there are many rooms in our father's house." The phrase "father's house" refers to heaven. The word *heaven* is used in two senses. It is the place where God is. It also refers to our eternal home where we shall be with God and all the saints when all things will be culminated in Christ. According to the first usage of the word, we foretaste heaven whenever we are in Christ. In Christ there are many rooms. If you want to be in Christ now, the door is wide open. According to the second usage of the term, Christ is telling us not to worry for we belong to the eternal home where we will fully experience God's love. In this beautiful city we will be free from our physical bodies, which are susceptible to worry and suffering. Our earthly suffering is temporary. But at the end of all things we will be where there is no more death, no more grief, or crying or pain.

We should not worry because Christ will come again. And he who will come has come. Nay, he is still coming; he will come at the end of time. There is no demarcation line between his first and second coming; he is simultaneously coming. Finally, he will come. At his first coming, he showed us the way to God. At his constant coming, he guides us through Holy Spirit. At his final coming, he will transform us in such a manner that we will not need to be shown the way.

We shouldn't let our hearts be troubled because Christ will take us to himself. He said, "I will come back and take you to myself so you will be where I am" (John 14:3). No earthly king can ever prepare a candidate who will be what he is or where he is. Christ is telling us not to worry because we will be as he is. We will share in his glory. We will have a spiritual body that will be like his body, which will never grow old, a body that will be out of the reach of AIDS, and a body that will never be subjected to material things. He who is coming has a good message of what you can do. He says, "I am telling you the truth: Whoever believes in me will do what I do. Yes, he will do even greater things, because I am going to the father" (John 14:12).

Finally, Christ is telling us not to worry because he is the way. He doesn't say that he is the road sign; he says that he is the way. He is not like a road sign, which can show you the way to Mobile, yet has never actually been there. He is the way to the Father. He is the true way because he came from the Father, has gone back to the Father, and his spirit is in us, guiding us to the Father. Since Christ is the true way to the Father, all that is required of us is to be in him. As long as we are in him we are on the right path. Thus, we have no reason for worrying about what will befall us. For those who are in Christ, God has a good plan for them. His word for us is don't worry. "I alone know the plans I have for you—plans to bring you prosperity not despair, plans to bring about the future you hope for" (Jeremiah 29:11).

CHAPTER SEVEN

The Resurrection And The Life

I am the resurr ection and the life—
come to me and pass from death to life.
—John 11:25

THE AFRICANS BELIEVE THAT DEATH opens the door to a superior life and that it is not the end but a beginning of life. We say, "To die is not to perish."

According to Kikuyu myth, when a person dies, he joins the departed in a place known as Menengai. For instance, when my maternal grandfather was very sick and awaiting this great opportunity, he used to tell me, "Gatungu, I am waiting for my passport for going to Menengai."

The Kikuyu believe that if you go to Menengai, you will see the "living dead" either grazing or working on the farm, but if you approach them they disappear. You cannot either touch them or communicate with them.

I once took an American friend to this holy spot. I told her about the departed who abide in the place. She was ready with a sophisticated camera.

After reaching the place, she said, "John, show me where they are, so that I can take their picture." I responded, "Put this camera down. Take the spiritual camera and use your spiritual eyes and you will have their pictures." Since she had no spiritual camera, she never took their pictures.

In this chapter, we explore how Christ is telling us that he is the continuation of life. He says, "I am the resurrection and the life. Whoever believes in me will live, even though he dies, and whoever lives and believes in me will never die" (John 11:25).

What is the meaning of resurrection? What is the meaning of life? The idea of resurrection of all people of the world was not developed in African religion or in Judaism. In the Old Testament, there is no explicit teaching about general resurrection. The idea of the resurrection in its fullest extent, both for the righteous and the wicked, was first found in Daniel: "Many of those who have already died will live again; some will enjoy eternal life, and some will suffer eternal disgrace" (Daniel 12:2).

But the belief in the general resurrection was prevalent in Jesus's time.

This is evident in Martha's dialogue with Jesus: "Your brother will rise to life," Jesus told Martha.

"I know," she replied, "that he will rise to life on the last day" (John 11:23–24).

After Martha's statement, Jesus claimed to be the resurrection, and since he was present, the resurrection was a present with him. He who will raise the dead one day is bringing resurrection here and now. The raising of Lazarus was proof that, "The time is coming, and now is when the dead will hear the voice of the Son of Man, and those who hear will come to life" (John 5:25).

As the first creation was through the Word, so will be the resurrection, which is the second creation. As the first Adam brought death to all humankind, so the second Adam will bring back to life all those who have died.

While the unbelievers will be raised for judgment, the believers will enjoy God's presence forever. The believers may suffer the earthly death, but they will have life in an ultimate sense. For those who are in Christ, there is no death in an ultimate sense. For them, death is unreal and is self-defeating, for it only opens the door to the glorious, endless life with God.

Through faith, we can start realizing this life here and now. "Whoever hears my words and believes in him who sent, has eternal life. He will not be judged, but has already passed form death to life" (John 5:24). Those who are in Christ, not only are their sins forgiven, but they are counted righteous here and now. They are cleaned from all unrighteousness.

The thoughts of their heart are cleansed by the inspiration of the Holy Spirit. They experience eternal life here and now.

The unbelievers are already judged and condemned. They are experiencing eternal death here and now. What does John mean by eternal life? John draws from his Jewish background and Philo's[21] idea of eternal life. As we have noted, the Jews had developed the idea of the age to come during the time of Jesus. That age was quantitatively and qualitatively different from this age.

According to Philo, this was the life of God. The life of God is not time, but eternity, which is the archetype of time. In eternity, nothing is past or future, but only present. For Philo, this eternity is "today," which is boundless and inexhaustible existence. It is free from periods of months and years. It is free from the notion of human reckoning by numbers. It is the very quality of God's existence, which is eternal and in the sense of timelessness. This is the existence of God, who is neither young nor old.

Who are enjoying eternal life? Who are experiencing eternal judgment and condemnation? "By their fruits ye shall know them" (Matthew 7:16).

Those who are condemned are the individuals who resist the love of God that is in Christ Jesus. The people who lock the third person of the Holy Trinity outside of their lives are those who expect everything from others and give nothing in return. They strive on socially useless sides. They strive for personal superiority regardless of social interest. They have no time for God and human beings. They bear no fruits that can sustain the community. Their characteristics can be summarized by a Kikuyu proverb: "He who eats alone, dies alone."

Dying alone was regarded as the greatest misfortune, and it was believed that this type of death resulted from a fruitless life. He who deprives others of himself is also deprived, and he who is deprived of others cannot live long.

Those who have eternal life are those who believe and live in Christ. These are people who bear good fruits. They are spiritually and socially healthy. They live in society. Their mode of life is so adaptable that, whether they want it or not, society derives a certain advantage from their work. These are people who contribute to furthering the kingdom of God.

I would like to ask you the following questions:

- On which side are you?

- Are you among those who bear good fruits?

- Are you among those who never rush on God's work because for you time belongs to God?

- Can you cancel important appointments because of God's work?

- Are you mindful of others?

- Does the society benefit from your work?

- Do you believe and live in Christ?

"I am telling you the truth," says Jesus. "whoever hears my words and believes in him who sent me has eternal life. He will not be judged, but has already passed from death to life" (John 5:24).

See Footnote 22.

CHAPTER EIGHT

The True Vine

I am the true vine—dwell in me

—John 15:1–17

"I AM THE TRUE VINE—DWELL in me." This statement depicts Christ as the true vine or the real vine. The word vine was translated by the church fathers as "vineyard." In this sense, Jesus and the Church are the vineyard. This imagery stems from the Old Testament where the Israelites are referred to as the vineyard. This symbol is used for Israelites in their relationship to God. In addition, the image of the tree is used in the same context and in the same sense as the vine. Thus, the statement, "I am the real vine," could also imply, "I am the real tree."

Interestingly, the symbol of a tree was used by the Africans to symbolize relationships to God. Most of the African people had a sacred tree under which God was worshipped. If there was a drought, the people gave sacrifices under these trees. A successful relationship of God and his people would result in the former answering the prayer and giving the people the rain immediately.

Some people attach their genesis to the tree. The Kikuyu people, for instance, traditionally believed that their first father, Kikuyu, emerged from the roots of the Mukuyu tree. If you visit Kenya, you can go to this holy place. There you would see two ageless trees. One of these trees, which is supposed to be male, has a straight trunk. The other has a protruded trunk resembling a pregnant woman and has a bottom similar to female reproductive organs. It was out of this hole, the myth tells, that God called the first man—Kikuyu.

Thus, the tree as a symbol delineates the relationship between God and his people. It is the meeting point between divinity and humanity. It is the object of our myths, stories, and riddles. It is indeed located in the center of humankind's Garden of Eden. In the deepest sense, the tree of God is a realm in our personality, which hungers and thirsts for the Holy Being. This realm remains restless unless it is filled with God.

Jesus is reminding us that he is the real tree. He is the real vine. We, the Church, are the branches. There are two types of branches. There are fruitful branches and fruitless branches.

What are the conditions of the fruitless branches? These are the disciples who are like Judas[22]—the type who are never assets but are liabilities to the Church. They are like the seeds that fell along the path and were eaten by the birds at once. They are like the seeds that fell among the thorn bushes

and never grew to bear fruits. These, of course, are the disciples who don't dwell in the vine. Consequently, they are cut off and thrown to the fire like the withered branches. To be out of Christ means self-condemnation. Thus, one cuts oneself from the flow of life.

How do we cut ourselves from the source of life? We cut ourselves by keeping aloof from the worshipping community. We then lose spiritual energy. If this separation is prolonged, the final result is spiritual death.

The church, like the branches in the vine, is a family institution. The sharing of the blood of Christ symbolizes a family structure that is consanguineous. This relation demands a regular attendance in the family meal and fellowship. As Luke tells us, the first branches "continued steadfastly in the apostles' doctrine and fellowship, and in breaking of bread and in prayers" (Acts 2:42).

What does it mean to be in the vine? To be in the vine means to dwell in Christ. This demands us to be in fellowship with other Christians. In this fellowship, God takes care of us as a gardener takes care of the vineyard. He prunes us in order for us to bear much fruit. Hence, there is no branch in the vine that doesn't bear fruit. Every member of a heathy family must have a particular role to play in the family.

To be in the real vine means being a perpetual disciple—always in Christ's college so as to learn about God day by day. And listening to God speaking to us daily through the community of faith, we become more aware of his will. And thus when we pray, God answers our prayers, because we pray in accordance to his will.

In the vine we learn to give our very selves just as Christ gave his life for us. As Jesus says, "The greatest love a person can have for his friends is to give his life for them" (John 15:13).

To this end, we need to ask ourselves the following questions:

- Can we stay alive without being in the vine?

- How can we claim to be in the true vine if we live away from other branches?

- How can we be members of the family if we don't have a regular face-to-face relationship with the member of the family?

- How can we be members of the family if we are irregular at the family's meal?

"I am the vine," says Jesus. "And you are the branches, whoever remains in me, and I in him, will bear much fruits, for you can do nothing without me" (John 15:5).

<u>22</u> All four Gospels agree that Judas Iscariot was one of Jesus's twelve disciples, and that he betrayed Jesus to the temple priests and guards. The betrayal began the final events leading to the crucifixion of Jesus. To be out of Christ means self-condemnation. Guilt led to the suicide of Judas.

CHAPTER NINE

The Eternal Word

Christ Jesus is the eternal word of God.

—John 1:1–14

THE PYGMY HAVE A TRADITIONAL hymn that describes God as word. They sing:

"In the beginning was God. Today is God.

Tomorrow will be God.

Who can make an image of God?

He has no body.

He is a **word**, which comes out of your mouth.

That word! It is no more.

It is past and still lives.

So is God!"

As this hymn delineates, God, who is the Word, was there in the beginning. Similarly, John tells us the Word (the Logos) was there from the beginning. This eternal word was at the roots of the universe and at the foundation of the world. He is the one who was, who is, and who is to come. He transcends time and space. As the pygmies describe him, he is a God who was there in the beginning. He is there today. He will be there tomorrow. His existence is different from other beings. Hence, no one can make an image of God. He is both supreme and unique.

In him and through him, all things were made. Independent of him, nothing was made. He is the archetype or primary pattern, according to which all things come into being. Since it is by him and through him that all things were made, he is the cooperating agent, the means and the end of their existence. Christ, the Logos, can impart the following qualities:

Quality No. 1. *Life.* In him was life and that life was the light of men. He is both the life and means of living. He came so that we might have life and have it in more abundance. This life is far more than a mere existence. It is the very presence of God dwelling in us and filling our lives with vitality. It means passing from death to life and being free from God's judgment. Whenever we enjoy "the dwelling of God" in us, we also enjoy justification—being counted righteous before God. We get this experience through faith in Christ. John tells us that his main purpose of writing the Gospel was, "that you may believe that Jesus is the Christ, the Son of God, and that by believing, you may have life in His name" (John 20:31).

If we have this life, do we need drugs or alcohol in order to feel high?

Quality No. 2. *The Light of the world.* Christ is the light that shines in the darkness. There has been war between the children of the light and the children of the darkness. The children of the darkness have attempted to put the light out, but have never succeeded.

Almost three decades ago I first preached and wrote that:

Christians have undergone persecution ever since the church was born. Right now in the Soviet Union there is a Christian who is being persecuted. In Ethiopia, where there is a Marxist government, Christians are being tortured. They are in prison because of their faith in Jesus Christ. Churches have been confiscated. There is no freedom of worship. Pastors are expected to have government permits for preaching and officiating, yet these permits are rarely granted. Despite the persecution, the church is growing by leaps and bounds in Ethiopia.

As I write today, the Ethiopian population remains two-thirds Christian.[23] "Thus, the light shines in the darkness and darkness has never put it out" (John 1:5).

Still, darkness has not disappeared. CNS News reported in February 2014:

Restrictions, harassment, and intimidation towards people who practice their religion increased in every major region of the world in 2012 except the Americas, with Christians the major target, says a new report by the Pew Research Center.

"Muslims and Jews experienced six-year highs in the number of countries in which they were harassed by national, provincial or local governments," the study found, but Christians continue to be the world's most oppressed religious group, with persecution against them reported in 110 countries.[24]

In July 2015, *The New York Times* newspaper was asking: "Is This the End of Christianity in the Middle East?: ISIS and other extremist movements across the region are enslaving, killing and uprooting Christians, with no aid in sight."[25] The more darkness fights against the light, the more the light shines. The more Christians are persecuted, the more they increase in number and strength. As Tertullian, an African apologist,[26] wrote to the Emperor who was persecuting the church, "The more you persecute us, the more we will spread. For the blood of the martyrs is the seed of the church."

When we are suffering because of our faith and when we are experiencing discrimination because of what we are, remember that God is on our side. Let us ever remember the words of Jesus. "But be brave! I have defeated the world" (John 16:33).

Quality No. 3. *Rebirth.* Those who believe in Christ are given power and the right of becoming God's children: "Not of the natural descent, nor the human decision or a husband's will, but born of God" (John 1:13).

Rebirth is a ritual that is prevalent in African culture. Through this ritual one was born to a family that was not his original family. After this rite, the initiate had all the privileges of a member of the family. An individual could also be born to another tribe, and, after the second birth, he became a full member of the tribe. Thus, we fully understand what it means to be born again.

However, in Christianity, we become God's children by believing in and receiving Christ. We are then born in the spiritual world. We became members of the Kingdom of God. As Jesus said to Nicodemus: "I tell you the truth, unless a man is born of water and the Spirit, he cannot enter the Kingdom of God, because that which is born of the flesh is flesh and that which is born of the Spirit is Spirit" (John 3:5).

Those who are born of the Spirit have desire for spiritual milk and food. They have a great appetite for reading God's Word and of being with God's people and being in God's house.

Quality No. 4. *Grace is another quality of the Logos.* The Word, which became all what we are except sin, was full of grace and truth. While the law was given through Moses, grace and truth came through Jesus Christ. The law reminds us of our misdeeds and our weaknesses. It shows us how we have missed the mark and makes us feel guilty. Grace makes us aware of the fact that we are invaluable, regardless of our deeds or misdeeds. In Christ, we are justified, and "From the fullness of his grace, we have received one blessing after another" (John 1:16).

In conclusion, Christ, as the Word, reminds us about the importance of communicating with God and with each other. Christ the light expects us to be real and genuine. He gives us the power and right of becoming God's children and challenges us to open all the windows of our beings so that we may filled with the life that flows from God himself.

23 Jayson Casper. Why Christians Are Fleeing One of Africa's Oldest and Largest Christian Homelands: Beyond the search for a better life, evangelicals and Orthodox in Ethiopia increasingly share even more. (June 18, 2015). Online as of December 2016 at http://www. christianitytoday.com/ct/2015/june-web-only/why-christians-are-fleeing-africa-ethiopia- orthodox.html

24 Barbara Boland. Pew Study: Christians Are The World's Most Oppressed Religious (February 6, 2014). Online as of December 2016 at: http://www.cnsnews.com/news/article/barbara-boland/pew-study-christians-are-world-s-most-oppressed-religious-group.

25 Eliza Griswold, Is This the End of Christianity in the Middle East?: ISIS and other extremist movements across the region are enslaving, killing and uprooting Christians, with no aid in sight. (July 22, 2015). Online as of December 2016 at: http://www.nytimes.com /2015/07/ 26/magazine/is-this-the-end-of-christianity-in-the-middle-east. html?_r=0.

26 Quintus Septimius Florens Tertullianus (AD 155–240), a Christian writer from Carthage in North Africa (then a Roman province).

CHAPTER TEN

The Humiliated And Exalted

Humiliated and Exalted Christ...

—Philippians 2:1–11

THE HUMILIATED AND EXALTED CHRIST makes a profound appeal to us because African history is that of marginalization and exaltation. We have been humiliated by colonialism. We have been marginalized by slavery. Our history and oral traditions have countless individuals who were mortified and exalted.

One of these individuals is the late president of Kenya, Jomo Kenyatta. Kenyatta was one of the first Kenyans to get a college degree. He lectured in the London School of Economics. He enjoyed a comfortable life in Europe for eighteen years. When he returned to Kenya, he was given a good job. Yet, he forsook this job and concentrated on mobilization of the Kenyan tribes to pull together and fight for freedom.

Thus, he posed a threat to the Britons. They labeled him a "communist" who intended to lead people to darkness. He was arrested and imprisoned in the remotest, hottest, and the most humid place in Kenya. There, he was tortured for eight years. The Bible and the Koran were the only books he was permitted to read.

After this suffering he was released, and eventually he became the first prime minister and the first president of Kenya. He is honored as one of the best African leaders and one of the founding fathers of Pan-Africanism and the Organization of African Unity.[27]

As it was with Kenyatta, Christ was humiliated and exalted. Although all things were created through him and for him, and although he is the Lord of the cosmos, and that it is in him that all things hold together, and, even though he was and is God, he emptied himself. He became a human being. How tiny did the Lord of the universe become? According to biologist, the fetus is as tiny as a *full stop*[28] in its first day in the womb. So God humbled Himself and became as tiny as a full stop. As though that was not enough, he took the form of a servant. The Greek word *servant* also means a slave. The Lord of all creation became a slave. "He humbled himself and became obedient to death, even death on the cross" (Philippians 2:8). As the suffering servant, He was despised and rejected by men; A man of sorrow and acquainted with grief; and as one form whom men hide their faces; he was despised, and we esteemed him not. Surely he has borne our griefs and carried our sorrows…He was wounded for our transgressions, he was bruised for our iniquities; upon him was the chastisement that made us whole and with his stripes we are healed. (Isaiah 53:3–5)

Here we have a God, who, like Kenyatta and indeed the black people, went to the liminal entity. He was despised. He was rejected. He was wounded. He was bruised. On the cross, he underwent physical and psychological suffering. He was on the cross wearing a crown of thorns for six hours—being burned by the hot sun of Palestine. Yet, he suffered because of healing the sick, feeding the hungry, and preaching the good news of the Kingdom of God. He loved his people so much. He gave his very self to them; and, they reciprocated by nailing him on the cross. He was, indeed, debased.[29]

Unlike Kenyatta, Christ was wounded for the transgressions of the whole world. He was humiliated to death, even death on a cross. However, the greater the suffering, the greater was his glorification. After death, he rose again with a spiritual and everlasting and non-aging body.

"God has highly exalted him and bestowed on him the name which is above every name and that at the name of Jesus, every knee should bow, in heaven and on earth and under the earth and every tongue confesses that Jesus Christ is Lord, to the glory of God the Father" (Philippians 2:9–11).

The humiliated and exalted Christ is our Christ. We have been despised. We are still being wounded for what we are. We have, nevertheless, been exalted. God, who is on the side of justice, has endowed upon us the special quality of life. Suffering and humiliation have produced human beings who are adaptable to change. This is an important quality of life since life itself is a flowing and changing phenomenon.

Lack of proper support from the oppressive status quo has compelled us to seek support from the Supreme Being. Consequently, the Supreme Being is with us in our worship and our daily living.

The presence of the Great Spirit in us has made our religion alive. In the words of Wallace Charles Smith, a black theologian, Black religious system…is alive. It is not a system that is a servant to print, media or linear logic. This liveliness provides a genuine opportunity for Black churches to base their theology on some novel premises.

By being segregated and excluded, we have developed an empathetic understanding of those who are excluded. We have developed a concept of inclusive community.

I remember an African theological student asking me, "How come, when we go to Europe and America, we experience culture shock, but when they come here, we don't suffer from the same experience?" My answer was, "Theirs is an exclusive community; ours is an inclusive community." The African culture, though possibly more complex than the Western culture, has a capacity for making every human being feel that he is an accepted member of the family. Africa, being the cradle of the human species, has a capacity for reclaiming all the sons and daughters of Adam. Christian missionaries succeeded in Africa because they were accepted and adopted as members of the African family.

A conference on Afro-Anglicanism held in Barbados in June 1985, attended by two hundred people of African descent from all over the world, epitomized black heritage and exaltation in Barbados. It affirmed that:

God has called us as Afro-Anglicans to be the salt of the earth, and that we are richly endowed with many gifts of grace and human virtues, to persevere in our Christian calling... We have endowments of warmth and feeling, of movement and beauty, of truthfulness and wisdom, of holism and familial responsibility of a spirituality of endurance and survival. [30]

Since we have these gift and virtues, let us, then, strengthen one another. Let us foster love, peace, and unity in our cities. Let us reach out and bring more people to the house of God. To this end, St. Paul is exhorting us, "If there is any encouragement in Christ, any incentive of love, any participation in the Spirit, any affection and sympathy, complete my joy by being of the same mind, having the same love, being in full accord and of one mind" (Philippians 2:1–2).

Amen.

27 President Kenyatta suffered a heart attack in 1966. In the mid-1970s, he lapsed into periodic comas lasting from a few hours to a few days from time to time. On 14 August 1978, he hosted his entire family, including his son Peter Magana who flew in from Britain with his family, at a reunion in Mombasa. On 22 August 1978, President Kenyatta died of natural causes attributable to old age; he was about eighty-six at the time of his death.

28 The *full stop* in the author's original Commonwealth English is known as the *period* punctuation mark in American English.

29 For the Gospel descriptions of the agony of the crucifixion, see Matthew 27:27–54; Mark 15:16– 39; Luke 23:26–47; and John 19:1–37.

30 Codrington Consensus, Conference on Afro-Anglicanism (October 29, 1985).

CHAPTER ELEVEN[31]

The Lord Of The Universe

Christ is the exalted king; serve him in love.

—Colossians 1:3–23

THE LECTTONARY DTRECTS OUR THOUGHTS to exalting Christ as the King. Nowhere else in the New Testament is Christ portrayed as the King of kings as in the epistle to the Colossians. Owing to this fact, John Calvin[32] describes the epistle as "an inestimable treasure." He says: "What is of greater importance in the whole system of heavenly doctrine than to have Christ drawn to the life, so that the fruits that accrue to us therefrom."

The significance of Colossians lies not only on its presentation of Christ as the King, but also on how he is related to God, to the Church, and to the universe.

In this respect, we can claim that this Christology has an African root. Christ is exalted in his divinity. In Africa, the Holy Being is put in the highest plane and is related to the cosmos. He is described as the Great One of the Forest, the All-Knowing, The Wise One, The Source of Wisdom, The Ancient of Days, The All-Powerful, The Sustainer, The Great Provider, the Being Who Is Self-Existence and Pre-Eminent. The Zulus address him as He Who is of Himself or He Who Comes of Himself into Being. The Kikuyu describe the being as The Unique Self or That Which Belongs to Itself. We say, "God has no father nor mother nor wife nor children; he is alone. He is neither a child nor an old man. He is the same today as he was yesterday."

Those of you who watched the TV program *The Africans* may ask, "Since God is highly exalted in Africa, why are there so many problems? Why is the continent threatened by constant economic and political instability?" I would like to draw your attention to the fact that the profound Christology of the epistle to the Colossians sprung out of a dangerous problem. It was written against a background of a heresy taught by unknown persons. These false teachers taught their followers to worship angels, celestial spirits, and cosmic powers. The heretics worshipped feast days, special seasons, and certain practices. These people were similar to some people in this society who worship themselves and TV programs. The worshippers of self and TV prefer giving devotion to self and the TV rather than to worshipping God, who is the sustainer and Creator of all things.

The author of the epistle to the Colossians reveals Christ as the divine agent of creation. All things were created through, by, and for him. "For through him God created everything in heaven and on earth, the seen and the unseen things including spiritual powers, lords, rulers, and authorities" (Colossians 1:16). Hence, all worship should be directed to God through Christ.

He is the principle of coherence for every creature. In him, all things hold together. He existed before all things (he is the ancient of the days) and in union with him all things have their proper place. He can cement the relationship between the members of a church family. He can harmonize the conflicting elements within yourself and give you the peace of God which passes all understanding.

Like the divine wisdom, or Logos, Christ is all pervasive. To use the New Testament writers' cosmology, the cosmic Christ came from the first world, he dwelt with the people of the second world, after death he descended to the third world, and after his resurrection he ascended into the first world. "He is the firstborn son who was raised from death in order that he alone might have the first place in all things" (Colossians 1:18). For that reason, if we worship God through Christ and in Christ's body, the church, we experience the fullness of God. Thus, his Spirit pervades the entire universe. In this capacity, he directs every process of life and every energy.

God, in his fullness, chose to dwell in Christ bodily. Christ is the Lord over all the angels, celestial beings, and all that is seen and unseen, and therefore we need to place value on him in our worship.

Furthermore, "He is the head of his body, the church; he is the source of the body's life" (Colossians 1:18). We should imitate him rather than imitating the church leader, because it is him and him alone who was and is sinless.

As we have seen, there are three threads that are interwoven and run through the "I am" statements of Christ and Christology of the New Testament. These threads are self-knowledge, self-giving, and intimacy. Christ, by having a deep self-knowledge, was able to give himself in love to the world. He in turn challenges us to know him that we may be able to know ourselves and consequently serve one another in love.

To this end, ask yourselves the following questions:

- Do you search yourself?

- Do you ask God to search you?

- Do you know yourself?

- Do you know your sins?

- Do you know your God?

- If you know yourself and your God, what is your special contribution to the family of God?

- What is your particular role in the family?

- If you happen to move from this city, or if you depart this world, what service will the family miss?

- If you go away, what will the people of this city miss?

Now pray this prayer: "Almighty and everlasting God whose will it is to restore all things in your well-beloved Son, the King of kings and Lord of lords, mercifully grant that the people of the earth, divided and enslaved by sin, may be freed and brought together under his most gracious rule, who lives and reigns with you and the Holy Spirit, one God, now and forever. Amen."

---

31 A lectionary lists a collection of scripture readings appointed for Christian and Judaic worship. Anglican, Catholic, and Episcopal (at least) lectionaries are designed to cover all the Bible verses over a three-year period.

32 John Calvin (10 July 1509–27 May 1564) was an influential French theologian and pastor during the Protestant Reformation. He was a principal figure in the development of the system of Christian theology later called Calvinism.

CHAPTER TWELVE

My Light And My Salvation

The Lord is my light and my salvation; whom shall I fear?

—*Psalm 27:1*

A CERTAIN MAN WAS DRIVING on a road that went through a thick forest full of gigantic elephants. Although many people feared to drive on this road, this man took courage and drove alone. Unfortunately, as he was approaching the middle of the jungle, he saw an elephant nursing its calf, standing in the center of the road. He took courage and drove near the elephant. The elephant stood stone still. She continued suckling her baby. The man drove nearer and nearer to the elephant. "This is a female elephant," the man said to himself. "It cannot hurt me." He drove closer and closer. He hooted louder and louder. As his car was just about to touch the baby elephant, the elephant seized the car and broke it into pieces. The man was crushed and died. The car never touched the baby elephant. If the baby elephant was a human being, he could have said, "My mother is my salvation; whom shall I fear? My mother is the stronghold of my life; of whom shall I be afraid?"

In the midst of constant war, in the midst of numerous enemies, David trusted the great protector; thus, he was able to say, "The Lord is my light, and my salvation; whom shall I fear? The Lord is the stronghold of my life. The Lord is my refuge; of whom shall I be afraid?" (Psalm 27:1). Whenever we are confronted with enemies, we should remember that the Lord is on our side. The Lord is all-powerful and all-knowing. He takes care of us just as the elephant takes care of her calf.

The psalmist doesn't deny the reality of the existence of the evildoers and enemies. Enemies are there. Man's enemies are as old as man himself. Our enemies are related to darkness. Thus, we learn to fear the darkness at the earliest stages of our life. Interestingly enough, the word *darkness* appears in the opening sentences of the creation story. "The earth was without form and void, and the darkness was upon the face of the deep" (Genesis 1:2).

The darkness, which is an enemy of mankind, existed before the creation. It is uncreated nothingness that opposes the created existence. It endeavors to prevent the movement of the Spirit and human freedom. It tries to put off the light that gives us the freedom of enjoying the divine peace and protection. Thus, for the psalmist, the Lord is first and foremost his light. "The Lord is my light and my salvation."

In his presence, the darkness vanishes. As we saw in the "I am" of Jesus, the light is one of the qualities of the eternal word. He is the light that shines in the darkness and the darkness did not overcome it. "The Lord is my light and my salvation; whom shall I fear?" He is our salvation. He can protect us as the elephant protected her calf. "The Lord is the stronghold of my life; of whom shall I be afraid?"

The Lord is our stronghold and our refuge, and therefore we have no reason for fearing our enemies. When evil men attack us, when evil men try to kill us, when evil men try to weaken our determination and aspiration, when evil men try to destroy our humanity, and when evil men try to weaken our egos they will stumble and fall. For the Lord is our stronghold and our refuge! The psalmist knew that he needed the Lord for his refuge and salvation, for he needed protection. He needed to be guarded not only from his enemies but from his loved ones. He was forsaken by his parents. "My father and mother have forsaken me, but the Lord will take care of me" (Psalm 27:10).

If you are forsaken by your father or your mother, if you are deserted by your spouse, if you are abandoned by your son or a daughter, or if you are forsaken by your intimate friends, you should always remember the Lord will take care of you. Remember to say with the psalmist, "The Lord is my light and my salvation; whom shall I fear? The Lord is my stronghold; of whom shall I be afraid?"

When we are confronted by enemies, we should never, ever run away from God, who is our salvation and our stronghold. We should run *to* God. We should say with the psalmist, "I have asked the Lord one thing; one thing only do I want; to live in the Lord's house all the days of my life, to marvel there at his goodness, and to ask for his guidance" (Psalm 27:4).

There, in the house of the Lord, you will find your mother and your father. In the house of the Lord, you will find your son and your daughter, and you will find your grandson and granddaughter. In the house of the Lord, you will find a brother and a sister. In the church you will find a friend. Through faith, you will find God himself. The Lord will shelter you and keep you safe. And instead of hooking your mind on your enemies, your mind will be cleansed by the inspiration of the Holy Spirit. Instead of singing for your enemies, you will sing of God. "Trust in the Lord. Have faith, do not despair. Trust in the Lord" (Psalm 27:14).

CHAPTER THIRTEEN

Prophet's Reward

ONE OF THE GREATEST LESSONS that I learned from our professor of pastoral theology at Vanderbilt University was about the reward of a true prophet. He taught us: "If you chose to be a true prophet, you must be ready to be treated as a true prophet." We had some member for whom the church was a religious club of the professionals. To this group, I was led by the Spirit to challenge them. I proclaimed the Gospel: "Unless one is born of the Holy Spirit, he cannot see the Kingdom of God." They challenged me and told me that I was preaching like a Baptist minister. A good number of them committed themselves to Christ and started a spiritual pilgrimage. They attended weekly Bible study and fellowship. However, some remained the same.

So, while we enjoyed a fruitful ministry and the love of the people of God in Pensacola City, Florida, the devil was plotting against us. He used the same method as he used with Joseph. The Bible tells us that God blessed Potiphar because of Joseph, his slave. His success attracted Potiphar's wife and she asked Joseph, "Come to bed with me." When he refused she had him put in prison (Genesis 39:1–23). In my case, Potiphar's wife tried to seduce me several times, but when she found that I was not yielding, she said, "I will put you on the street." I didn't understand what she meant by putting me on the street.

About this time, the first edition of *Christ and Roots* had been published. This coincided with a Diocesan Clergy Conference. So, joyfully and naively I presented the book to the bishop and asked him to mention the book to the clergy. His face turned red and he remarked, "So you spend all your time writing books instead of ministering the parish?" From that time, he was looking for ways to get rid of me. This incident was followed by an Episcopal visitation. The seductive woman had an audience with the bishop.

She accused me of African-ness and accent. The following day she gave me a call and said, "Father, forgive me for lying to the bishop about you."

I asked, "Could you pick up the same phone and tell the bishop that you lied to him?"

She retorted, "Sorry, I don't have the courage to do so." The following day I found she had left a present for me in the office.

After this incident, I was invited by the bishop to his office. I took my wife, Mary, with me. The bishop quickly came to the point. With a heavy Southern accent, he said, " You have to go because of two things, "African- ness and accent."

After the judgment, Mary held the bishop by the shoulders and said, "Bishop, let me ask you a question."

"Yes, Mary," responded the bishop. "Are you a Christian?"

"Yes, I am," said the bishop."

"If you are a Christian, be listening to good people and not to bad people.

It can be cold there. Be a shepherd to your priest."

On this note, we left the bishop and we never saw him again.

After this, one of the Wise Virgins,[33] who was a professor, visited with the bishop and asked him why he had fired their priest. "It is not me, it is the Church Council," he claimed. Then she confronted the Church Council and they said, "It is not us, it is bishop."

What amazes me is that even though we were misjudged, we were not angry with the bishop or the church. We had a clear conscious for having done what the Lord wanted us to do. We felt fulfilled for the way God used the gifts he had given us. And, indeed, we gave only what we received from God and the church. As the following testimonies from the senior warden and altar director indicate, we developed the congregation by starting and empowering several programs: youth programs, Women of the Church, men's fellowship, and Bible studies that met in the church and homes. We connected the church to spiritual movements such as Kairos and Cursillo. Mary and I, having been brought up in an ecumenical city, Nakuru, Kenya, were ministers of all people of God in the city.

We did the following:

MOTIVATION PROGRAMS FOR COLLEGE BOUND

We invited African and African-American professors from the University of West Florida and Pensacola Junior College to motivate the community. They all made great presentations on the importance of education. Consequently, a good number of participants enrolled in the college and university. Consequently, I was invited to motivate students in middle schools and high schools.

DIALOGUE BETWEEN POLICE OFFICERS AND THE COMMUNITY

In those days, Pensacola ranked number six in crime in Florida. We were led by the Spirit to bring together law enforcement officers and citizens. We even invited the criminals. But humorously, instead of attending the dialogue, they stuck their hair in the door to the parish hall where the meeting was taking place. Many useful questions were raised, such as, "Someone is breaking in the door, and when I call 911, you have to keep on asking questions instead of coming at once. Why do you do this?" A police officer answered, "When you call, we start driving to your home immediately, but we keep you on the phone so as to know what is going on." At the end of the session, there was a better understanding between the officers and the community.

WE ALSO TAUGHT IN PENSACOLA JUNIOR COLLEGE in the Department of Humanities. Courses included: Humanity in the Ancient World, Humanity in Modern World, Humanity and Art. I had two classes. One of the classes had civilian students. The other was for military students at the naval and air bases. I was surprised to note that the military students did better than the civilians. They were also more adventurous. For instance, in a class on Humanity and Art, they asked me whether they could visit our home for dinner so that they might see African arts in food. I told them that I had to ask my wife because that was her department. Reporting to Mary, she told me that she would also like to see the American art in cooking. So we decided to have a covered dish featuring American and African foods. To motivate my daughter to join the navy, I asked that a few of them come in navy uniforms. We enjoyed cerebrating with African and American food. Henceforth, our daughter's greatest desire was to join the navy. She did this after graduating from high school.

BREAKING CULTURAL BARRIERS was another ministry that the Creator entrusted to us. In my office we had weekly fellowship with two Anglo priests. Most of the time we were so surprised to note we had related blessings and challenges. On one occasion, the Loving Father accorded me a humorous episode. A white priest who was going on vacation asked me to supply for him. In his church there was a parishioner who vowed that he could not take communion from a black priest. However, lovely men attended the church. After service, the generous church members took me out for lunch. This new friend happened to sit next to me at the table. Then a humorous man revealed the secret to me.

"Father, the man sitting next to you had said that he cannot take communion from a black priest; we were so surprised that he took communion from you."

"I particularly came because of him," I responded.

He responded, "When I saw you, I said, 'Ministerial alliance' is here. But when you preached I had a different view. I said to myself, I wish our priest could stay away longer so that we can have more of you."

I hugged the man and since then he became a new creation.

HEALING was another ministry that the Great Physician did through us. We had two girls who were afraid of water. Deed was eleven years old and was in baptism class. She was better than other children in memorizing The Apostles' Creed, the Ten Commandments, and Bible verses. But any time we had a baptism, she could not come to church. I asked her mother what she did when she needed a shower. "It is always a battle," said the mother.

Mary and I visited the family at their home. I asked Deed to sit with me. I

asked her, "Do you believe in God the Father, God the Son, and God the Holy Spirit?"

"I do," she responded."

"Do you want to be baptized in the name of the Father and the Son and the Holy Spirit?"

"I do."

"With warm or cold water?" "It does not matter."

I then asked for water and baptized the girl. Tears were rolling down her cheeks. A few days later, I received a card stating: "Thank you, Father Githiga, for baptizing me." I have baptized thousands of Christians, but she was the only person who has written a thank-you card.

The other miracle was a ministry to thirteen-year-old Tumika. I noted her hydrophobia when we were crossing the bridge to Pensacola Beach, which is three miles long. Approaching the bridge, Tumika shouted, "Water!" and started shivering. So on Sunday after church we took her and other youth to our home. I then asked her to come with me to the kitchen sink. I opened the faucet and told her, "This is the same as the water at the beach. It is harmless. I will pour some water on your hands, and I want you to trust that it is not going to hurt you." So I poured the water and I could see God healing the girl. After this, we took her and other youth to the beach. To our great surprise, Tumika was first to dash to the water. Her fear of water vanished completely.

God did many other great works through us, but we have shared these so as to encourage the many servants of God who have been betrayed, so they may know they are not alone. God will bless the seed they have planted, and there are faithful people of God who see and appreciate your ministry. Better still, if you are being betrayed and finally thrown from the pulpit, do not curse the church. Bless the church! This is what we did in our farewell message.

DR. GITHIGA'S FAREWELL MESSAGE

As I look toward our departure, which is at hand, I expressed my gratitude to Almighty God, who called us to come and minister at St. Cyprian's Church in Pensacola, Florida. The Supreme Being had planned our being together before the foundation of the world. I greatly praise the Giver of all things for the way he has used the gifts which he has given me and my family. I am grateful to my family who has willingly ministered with me.

Mary has transported the members who had no transportation. She has sung in the choir, worked with Altar Guild, and youth, strengthened spirits of the men of the church, and reminded me about small details such as putting the hymn numbers on the board and the prayers for the birthdays.

Rehema has participated in Junior Chair and youth program; she calls young people on Tuesdays, reminding them of the choir practice and youth program. She started a nursery for babies.

Isaac Cyprian has attracted more babies to St. Cyprian's. He has, however, the propensity of attracting more girls than boys.

My tremendous appreciation goes to the Church of God at St. Cyprian's Church. These faithful Christians, ecclesia in ecclesia, have given us moral support, useful advice, and encouragement. They have indeed been pastors to us. We have always felt loved and taken care of. I have never felt discriminated against by the church in the church on the basis of my personality type or nationality or accent. This church, being the creation of the Holy Spirit, has discerned, cherished, and used our gifts of the Spirit. She has indeed appreciated our gifts and drawn from the wealth of our spirituality. I will ever be grateful to the church, which has boldly enthroned Christ.

It is my prayer that God will continue to sustain, guide, illumine, and keep his church after our departure. Our separation is temporary since at the end of all things we will dwell in our Father's house forever. Since my contract expires on August 31, I will take my annual leave on August 1. My family will be leaving toward the end of August. If I don't have a job in this country, I will depart a few months after August.

May the peace of God be with you and remain with you always. The Rev. Dr. John G. Githiga, May 12, 1991

The following testimonials highlight how we were perceived by the church in Pensacola, Florida, and by Bishop George Njuguna who was our bishop before we left for United States:

RECOMMENDATION FROM ALTAR DIRECTOR:

TO WHOM IT MAY CONCERM

My name is Helen Edwards. I have been a member of St. Cyprian's Episcopal Church for thirty-five years. I am writing this letter on behalf of the Rev. Dr. John Githiga who has served as our vicar for five years. During his tenure at St. Cyprian's, I have observed many positive changes, such as the reactivation of men's club and Episcopal Church women's organization, an increase in Sunday and mid-week church attendance, an increase in member participation in Diocesan activities at Camp Beckwith and summer camp for youth, and the establishment of an Altar Guild and children's choir. Rev. Githiga has been responsible for organizing weekly Bible study and prayer groups. He has encouraged church to attend Cursillo activities and other Diocesan workshops and seminars. I strongly feel that Rev. Githiga' s sermons exemplify his profound ability to preach and teach. Also, he routinely ministers to the sick and shut-ins. As Altar Guide Directress, I have had the privilege of working closely with Rev. Githiga. He has exhibited an even temper, which has been very necessary, as he worked with the diverse groups of communicants at St. Cyprian's Church. It is my pleasure to recommend the Rev. John G. Githiga as highly capable of fulfilling any position for which he may apply.

Sincerely, Helen Edwards

FROM THE SENOR WARDEN

July 14, 1991

TO WHOM IT MAY CONCERN:

It is my pleasure to submit this letter recommending the Rev. Dr. John Githiga as a potential rector of your parish.

As a long time communicant, lay reader, holder of various positions of responsibility and, ultimately, senior warden in St.

Cyprian's Episcopal Church, I have had opportunity to work and observe Dr. Githiga during the last five years. Dr. Githiga brought to this church a wealth of leadership qualities that proved to be beneficial to this congregation over the last five years.

In church development, Dr. Githiga revived youth interest in the church through special youth programs including youth reading of the lectionary on a regular basis on one Sunday of the month throughout each calendar year. Under his leadership, active membership attendance increased during the past five years. Lay participation in services increased proportionately. Through his guidance, I have become more proficient in understanding and aiding in the administration of the lay ministry as well as performing other duties assigned to me during his tenure. I am sure that I speak for a majority of this church when I say that we regret the financial situation[34] at this time prohibits our retaining Dr. Githiga as vicar and wish him success in being situated elsewhere in a deserving role of employment.

Sincerely,

Joseph F Young, Jr. Senior Warden

FROM DOCTRAL STUDENT GRAMBLING STATE UNIVERSITY

P.O. Box 3296 Grambling State University

Grambling, LA 71245

TO WHOM IT MAY CONCERN:

Dear Sir, I find Dr. John Githiga to be a highly intelligent theologian! I am impressed by his keen insight and his ability to use God's word as a tool to solve the complex problems of modern society. Dr. Githiga adds an Afro-centric approach to the Scriptures. He accomplishes this without compromising God's love and concern for all mankind. Since I have been admitted to Doctoral Studies at Grambling, I have benefited from his counseling and ministerial services. Furthermore, Dr. Githiga allows his members to express their opinions without compromising church or spiritual doctrines. He reminds me of men like Elijah and Daniel in his prophetic ministry. I view Father Githiga as an asset to God, church, and humanity! Therefore, I am honored to recommend him for your services.

Respectfully, Tommy Johnson

FROM GRAMBLING STATE UNIVERSITY

Certificate of Recognition and Appreciation

Presented to

The Reverend John Githiga

In Recognition and Appreciation of your outstanding contribution in promoting International Awareness and cultural Diversity at Grambling State University.

March 6–10, 1995

International Week

Division of Student Affairs,

Grambling State University,

Grambling, Louisiana

Given this 8th day of March, 1995

FROM THE BISHOP OF MT. KENYA SOUTH

CHURCH OF THE PROVINE OF KENYA DIOCESE OF MT. KENYA SOUTH

P.O. Box 23030 Lower Kabete 7 August 1991

TO WHOM IT MAY CONCERN:

I have known Dr. John Githiga for a period of not less than twenty-five years. I knew him when he was a young man and very active in church activities. He went to Church Army College and when he finished we worked together as a Diocesan Youth advisor. He stayed in my parish and we shared the same office. He was very active, creative, and uplifted the standard of our youth so much that in inter-diocesan youth conferences, we were recognized as good in knowing our Bible. We defeated other youth groups in Bible knowledge, drama, and game competitions. He was involved in producing a book, *Ewe Kijana* ("Oh Young Man"), which we still use here on youth activities.

When Dr. Githiga became a pastor after training at St. Paul's United Theological College, we worked together in the Diocese of Nakuru and when I finished my studies in America, I joined him at St. Paul's United Theological College where the two of us were tutors.

He was heading the Department of Pastoral Theology. When I became a bishop in 1984, I invited him to work in my Diocese where he cared for more than three thousand Christians. People loved him for his creativity, humility, and pastoral concern for all people. He was good at pastoral visitation, organizing courses for elders, youth, and Mothers' Union, Sunday school teachers, and others.

Mrs. Mary Githiga started a group of young children known as Boys and Girls Brigade. She was good at leading Mothers' Union, uplifting their standards in child care, cookery, health care, and Bible studies. Both Dr. and Mrs. Githiga are people I can recommend very highly for any kind of work in the church.

As the recommendations indicate, our fruitful ministry is due to the dedication of Mary. She was fully involved in ministry long before we were married. She has been involved in children, youth, women, prison, hospice ministries, and praise and worship in the church. The article from *The Canyon News* highlights her commitment:

HOSPICE HONORS GITHIGA

Mary Githiga was honored and presented a certificate of appreciation on April 20, 2012 by BSA Home Care and Hospice. The certificate was for 10 years of dedicated service to the patients and families of BSA Home Care and Hospice. Githiga volunteers to give pastoral care to the terminally ill and the dying. She also volunteers as a Greeter in TEXAS during the summer and as minister at St. Cyprian's International Church in Amarillo. She hosts a Bible study group, which meet at their home. Mary is a comforter and encourager and likes comforting the patients and their families. She and her husband has lived in Canyon for 16 years.

The Parable of the Ten Virgins, also known as the Parable of the Wise and Foolish Virgins, is one of the parables of Jesus. According to the Gospel of Matthew 25:1–13, the five virgins who are prepared for the bridegroom's arrival are rewarded, while the five who are not prepared are disowned. The parable has a clear theme: be prepared for the Day of Judgment. John Barton, *The Oxford Bible Commentary*, Oxford University Press, 2001.

Financial problems were a rationalization from the Diocesan office. After five years, the church has grown in membership, participation, mission, and stewardship. We paid Diocesan apportionment on time and we also got our compensation on time. This is why the bishop told us, "You have to go because of your Africanness and accent."

CONCLUSION

IN CONCLUSION, WE ARE FULLY convinced that in all things, God is in control and has our best interest at heart. I fully agree with St. Paul: "All things work together for good to those who love God and are called for His Purpose" (Romans 8:28). For the last fifty-six years I have served him, I am awed by the way he has directed the events of our lives. His timing is perfect. At the time, we thought we were dying; it was the very time we were being born to a fuller life. And fuller freedom of service.

Amazingly, my last sermon at St. Cyprian's was on July 27, 1991, which was exactly my birthday. And on July 27, 2007 (my birthday), All Nations Anglican Church was incorporated in the State of Texas, and the following year we were given 501 c 3 status, which was backdated July 27, 2007. To embrace all the people of God, ANAC was renamed All Nations Christian Church International, home of All Nations Anglican Church. For more information, visit <allnationscci.org> and watch ANCCI TV on youtube.com.

As I write this conclusion, we are in over seventy countries with over two million members. Most, if not all, of our affiliates have gone through what we have gone through. As their chief servant, they have given me many titles, which include: Padre, Abuna, Bis, Bishop, Archbishop, Papa, and Patriarch (I was first called Patriarch in Sudan). The titles Padre, Abuna, and Papa, all of which mean "father," were first given me by my mother and the midwife (who was grandmother on my mother's side). When I was born, my grandmother reported to my father: "We have seen men and it is your father-in-law," which means that I was born as an individual and as community and for the community.

I was first named bishop by my fellow students at Nakuru Youth Club where I was training as a painter and sign writer. They gave this title because I was the one who taught them religious education at the age of eighteen years. I was formally consecrated as bishop by Hartley Ward, Archbishop of Anglican Church Worldwide, on all Saints Sunday to signify that I was called to minister all saints. This is the communion that the apostle John saw: "After this I looked, and there before me was a great multitude that no one could count, from every nation, tribe, people and languages standing before the throne and in front of the Lamb they were wearing white robes and holding palm branches in their hands and they cried with a loud voice: Salvation belong to the Lord our God who sits on the throne, and to the lamb" (Revelation 7:9–10).

I was consecrated Archbishop at a Native American Reservation. I was named Patriarch when I was in mission in Southern Sudan. Naming and ordination rites symbolizes the fact that I am called to minister to the people of all social strata—the rich and the poor, the educated, and the people who cannot read in any language. My other official title is John XIII. This means that in our Apostolic succession, which goes back to St. Peter, there were twelve patriarchs who were named John. Interestingly, *Patriarch* is officially addressed: "Your Beatitude," which symbolizes the community for which he is a chief shepherd.

Jesus talked about this community this way:

Blessed are the poor, for theirs is the Kingdom of heaven. Blessed are they who mourn, for they will be comforted. Blessed are the meek, for they will inherit the earth.

Blessed are those who hunger and thirst for righteousness, for they will be filled. Blessed are the merciful, for they will receive mercy.

Blessed are pure in heart, for they will see God.

Blessed are the peacemakers, for they will be called sons of God. Blessed are those who are persecuted because of righteousness, For theirs is the Kingdom of heaven (Matthew 5:3-10).

I must admit that I have experienced most of the things mentioned in the beatitude.

I grew as an orphan during the war and we indeed experienced hunger. There was a time when my mother had to measure the portion of food by her palm. The very country in which I was named Patriarch was the place where my bishop and I experienced poverty. By being merciful to the poor community, we gave all that we had. Reaching Juba to board the plane to Kenya, our tickets were not found in their computer. We were required to pay $600 but had only $125. And the $100 note was too old to be accepted within Sudan or Kenya. We spent the whole day at the airport poor and hungry. We had to beg a taxi to take us to a motel. When in the motel we had to beg to the very people we had given what we had. My companion became very sick. We became beggars. As I explain in *Ministry to All Nations*, we were forced to marry Lady Poverty. We begged at Juba Airport. I begged from a Sudanese American who was sitting with me in the plane.

I mourn for my international brothers and sisters who are going through persecution in India, Pakistan, Syrian, and Nigeria. I cry almost every day about Haiti. As you can see from the preceding chapter, we have been persecuted for doing what God has commanded us to do. But what we have gone through does not compare with the peace and joy of the Lord. We experience a lot of grace.

Thus, Jesus has enjoyed fulfilling his promises: "No one who has left home or brothers or sisters or mother or father or children and fields for me and the Gospel, will fail to receive a hundred times as much in this present age (home, brothers, sisters, mothers, children and fields—along with persecutions—and in the age to come eternal life" (Mark 10:29–30).

ABOUT THE AUTHOR

Dr. Githiga is Patriarch of All Nations Christian Church International; Archbishop, All Nations Anglican Church; Chancellor at ANCCI University; former chaplain and faculty at West Texas A&M University, Grambling State University, Pensacola Junior College, and St. Paul's University; founder and president of the African Association for Pastoral Study and Counseling. He is a graduate from Church Army College, St. Paul's University, Makerere University, the University of the South, Vanderbilt University, and International Bible Institute and Seminary. He holds Dip. Th, M.Div., D. Min, DRE, DD degrees. He appeared in the 2008–2009 edition of the *Madison Who's Who Registry of Executives and Professionals,* having demonstrated exemplary achievement and distinguished contributions to the business community. He is married to the Rev. Dr. Mary Githiga.

OTHER BOOKS BY THE AUTHOR

The Spirit in the Black Soul Holy Spirit:

The Greatest Promise and the Greatest Gift of All

Initiation and Pastoral Psychology: Toward African Personality Theory

Ministry to All Nations:

Practical Theology of Mission and Church Planting

The Secrets of Success in Marriage

www.ingramcontent.com/pod-product-compliance
Lightning Source LLC
Chambersburg PA
CBHW021004150626
46549CB00012BA/1083